AF375279

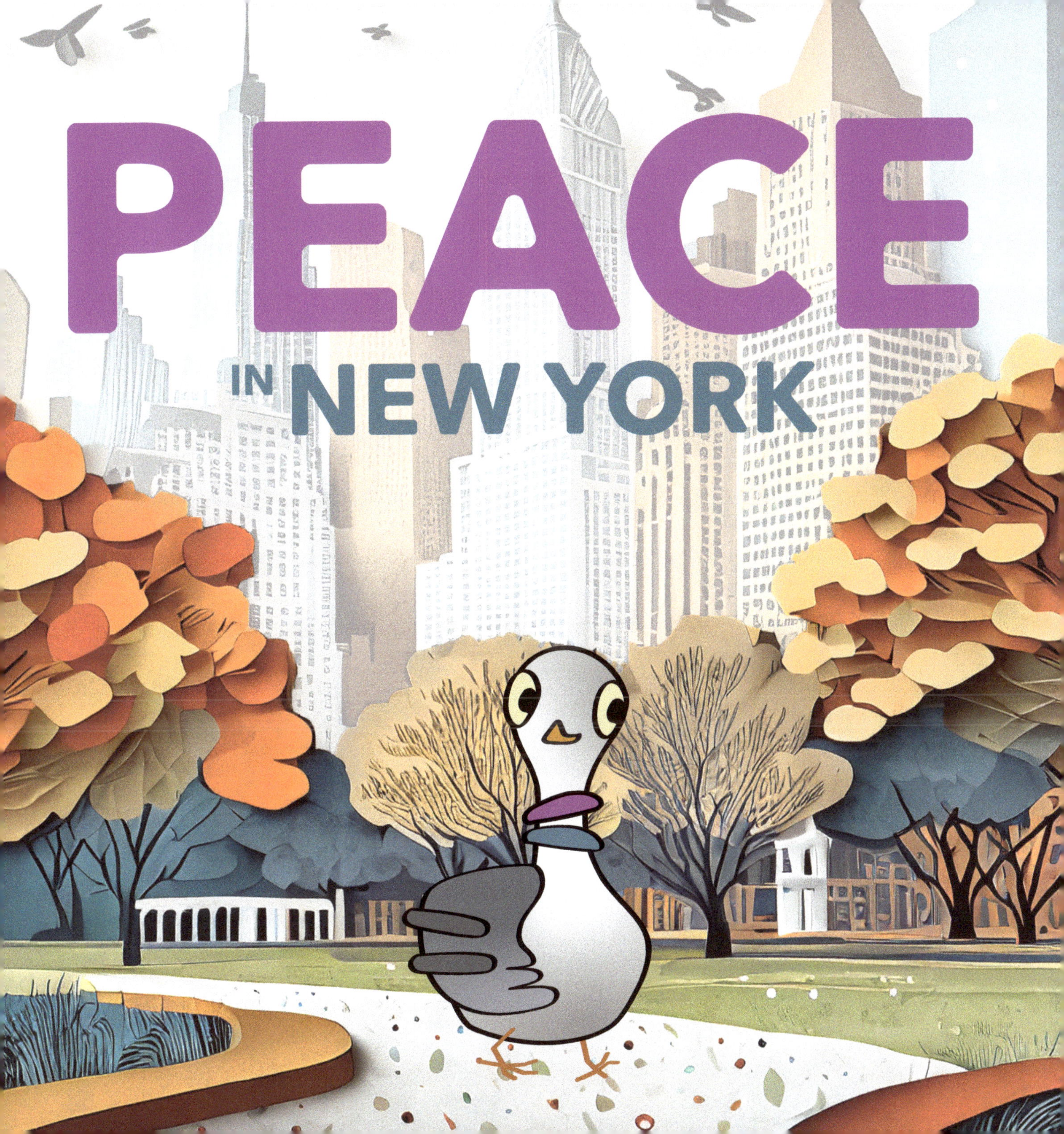
PEACE
IN NEW YORK

For my family:
Irene Kang and Su Jang
Woohyon Kang and Yun Kyoung Jung
Young Tae Chang and Ok Soon Lee

The background illustrations were
co-created with Adobe FireFly

Published in the United States by Doodle Thinking

ISBN: 979-8-8690-3656-8

This book belongs to:

In the heart of New York
City's magical Madison Square
Park, where trees stood tall
and flowers filled the air with
sweet smells, lived a very
special pigeon named Peace.

Her feathers sparkled like
silk, and her eyes twinkled
like stars in the night sky.
Peace wasn't just any bird,
she was extraordinary.

Hi! I'm Peace. Madison Square Park is my wonderful home.

Peace loved the lively park. She adored the sound of children laughing and playing on the playground, the whimsical tunes of street performers, and playful squirrels hopping among the trees.

Uh-oh! Peace was really surprised! When Peace and her pigeon friends tried to eat yummy crumbs that their kid friends shared, some people chased them away. So, Peace and her friends needed to find a safe place on the branches of trees.

How can we live together joyfully?

Peace hurried to gather all the pigeons in Madison Square Park and chat about what just happened. She flew up and perched on an old statue to begin the discussion. Pigeons from both the treetops and the ground joined in, curious about the topic.

What ideas do we have to make our park really, really amazing?

People don't seem to notice how awesome we are.
Coo-coo!
Maybe they think we're pigeons from outer space!
We're just like them, living in this concrete jungle.

If we wear costumes like superheroes, could we be friends?
People might love our feathered hero capes!
What's our pigeon superpower?

As the pigeons discussed,
a soft voice joined the
conversation. It was
Flora, a lovely flower who
had been listening nearby.

Hi, friends! I'm Flora. Ever wonder why people really love bees, even though bees can sometimes be a little bit aggressive?

I believe it's because people might get a little nervous around them. Do you think people might be cautious about bees because of their stings?

Yes, that could be it. But people also like bees because they're like tiny superheroes too! They zip around, pollinate flowers, and make gardens bloom. They spread joy and happiness.

Flora, you have such a sweet scent, and your colorful petals are so delightful. People may love you for that.

Hahaha. Thank you. I think people like us because we deliver messages that words can't say for their special ones. Just like you did in the past.

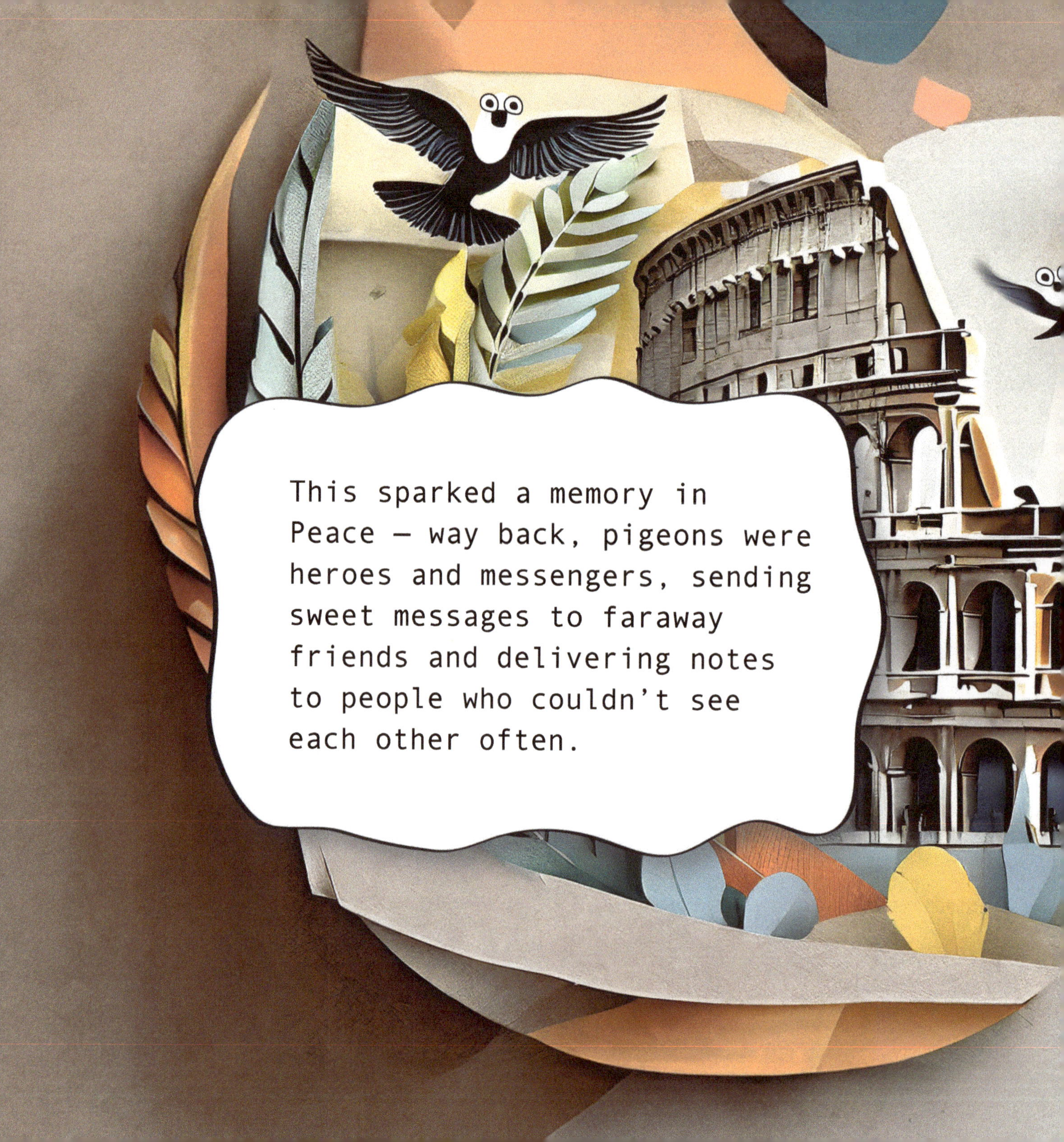
This sparked a memory in Peace — way back, pigeons were heroes and messengers, sending sweet messages to faraway friends and delivering notes to people who couldn't see each other often.

What if we become messengers again, sharing words that make hearts happy? We can make people smile and give them unforgettable memories.

Peace overheard a delivery person talking on the phone, sounding a bit worried.

"I have so many mails to deliver to the other side of the park, and they need to be there today. What should I do?"

Peace eagerly asked the delivery person, "We can zoom through the sky and deliver these messages with no traffic. Can we help?"

The delivery person was super happy to get help delivering everything on time!

A child, holding a mail delivered by Peace, came over with sparkling eyes.

"Thank you for delivering the lovely message from my grandpa! This is what I've been waiting for. You made my day!"

Keep spreading inspiration in your world!

IRENE

It's for you! We want to make people happy and bring peace to their hearts.

ZZZz
ZZZz

Peace, feeling content and joyful, found a cozy spot on a tree branch. As the sun dipped low in the sky, she closed her eyes for a little nap. In her dreams, a magical world unfolded.

The park changed. The people of Madison Square Park created a special area in the park, inspired by the joy Peace and her friends brought. They built a pigeon statue, adorned with symbols of peace.

When Peace woke up, she couldn't believe her eyes. The park had indeed transformed into the harmonious and happy place she had dreamed of. It was a world where everyone was kind and understood each other.

People stopped, smiled, and eagerly awaited the pigeon messengers. Peace and her friends couldn't believe their eyes.

This is the world we made together.

OTHER BOOKS
BY JUNE KANG

Our First Dance: Daddyhood Journey with Doodle Thinking

"An attractive, if flawed, a board book that may still spark parental creativity."

Kirkus Reviews

Explore limitless creativity through Doodle Thinking! It's a natural process that enhances creative and logical thinking by allowing you to draw what you imagine. 'Our First Dance' visualizes the positive impact of parenthood using creative doodles, aiming to foster empathy in children. The book encourages fathers to share their daddyhood journeys, unlocking creativity through Doodle Thinking. Join the journey, share stories, and inspire creativity with your kids.

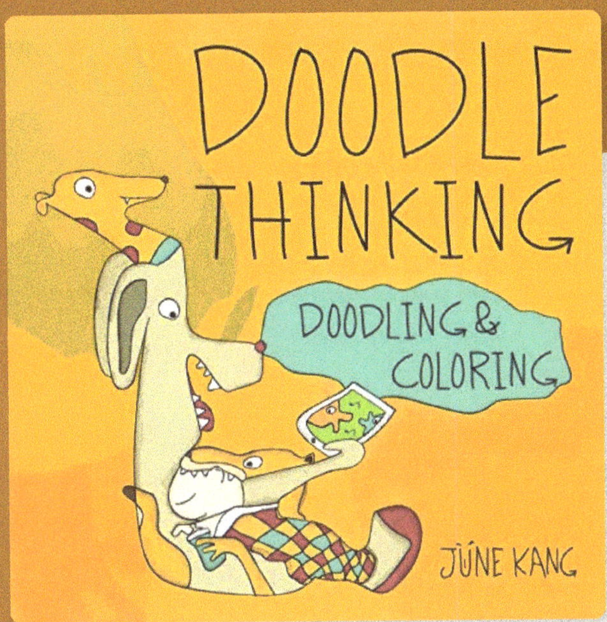

> "The 'Doodle Thinking' mantra is a fun approach to drawing that aims to really fire up both brain hemispheres with some abstract creativity."

Words and Illustrations

Doodle Thinking: Doodling and Coloring Book

Doodle Thinking taps into your natural creativity, training you to embrace ambiguity and unleash your inner genius. It's for kids, friends, and you! Connect your creative and logical brains, unlock original thinking, and bring dreams to life with random shapes. The book inspires with 60 on-the-go doodling and coloring pages, inviting you to embrace challenges, draw, color, and frame your masterpieces. Experience the simplicity of Doodle Thinking unlocking your creativity effortlessly.

A big thank you to my daughter, Irene, for helping make the storyline better with great advice on the narrative. Also, a special thanks to my wife, Suhyun, for her good ideas about the whole concept.

I owe a huge thanks to my father, Woohyon, whose daily inspiration and actions have been an endless source of motivation for me. Additionally, my heartfelt thanks to my mother, mother-in-law, and father-in-law for their support and encouragement throughout this journey.

Peace in New York
The Undiscovered Pigeon Tale in New York